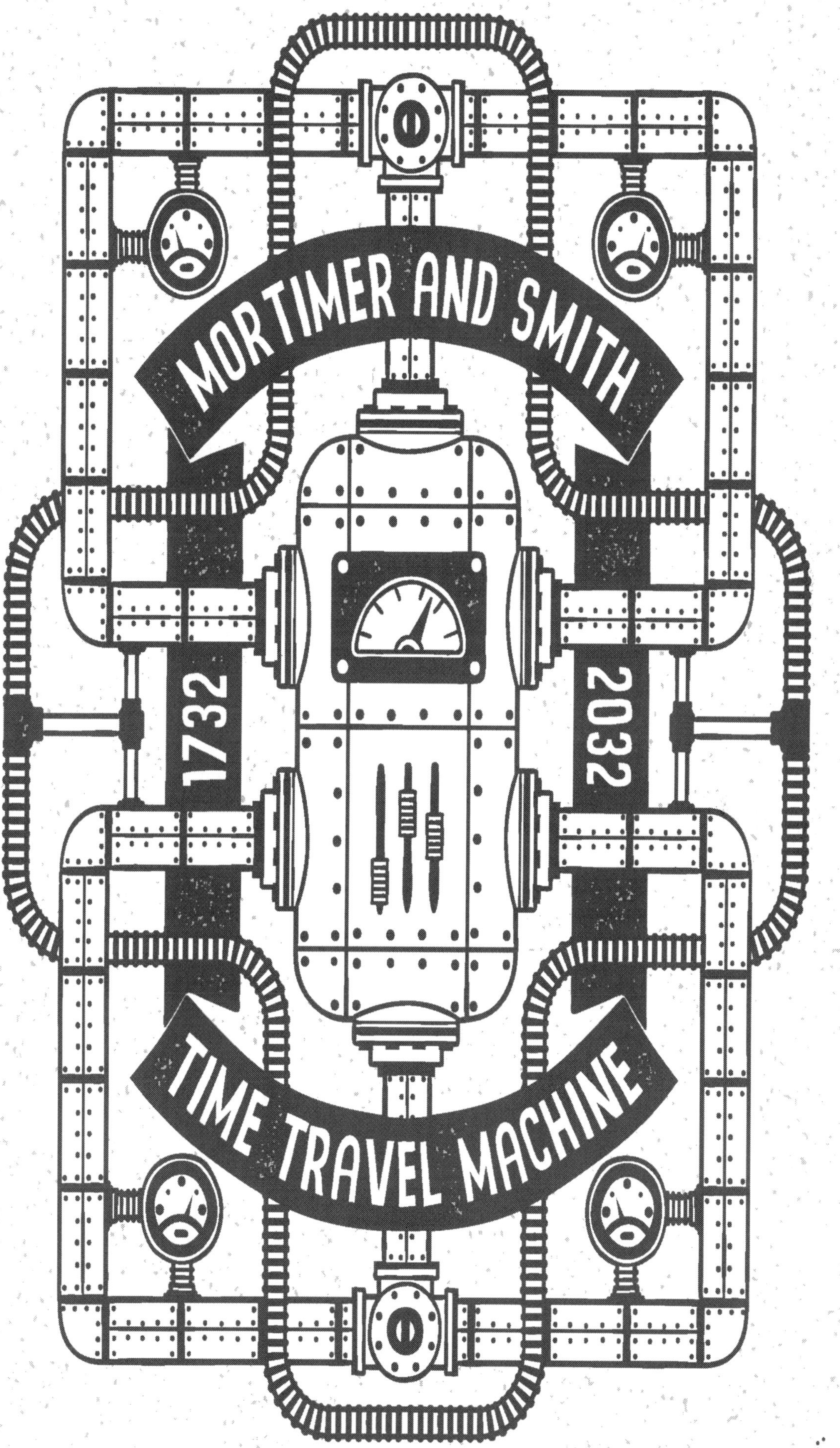
MORTIMER AND SMITH
1732
2032
TIME TRAVEL MACHINE

12
1
2
3

XII
I
II
III
IIII
V
VI
VII
VIII
IX
X
XI

SECOND SET OF PAGES

BEGINS HERE

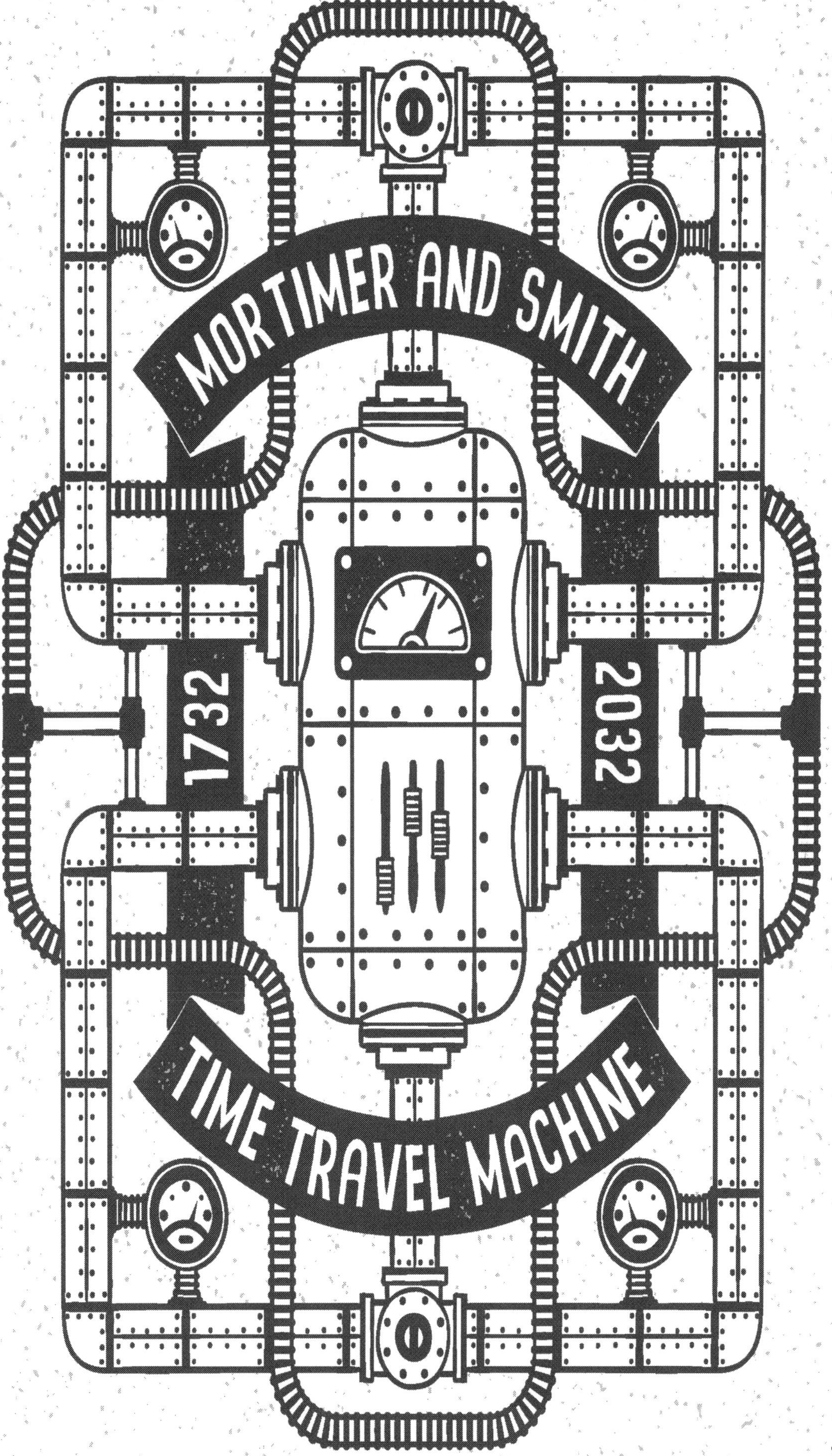
MORTIMER AND SMITH
1732
2032
TIME TRAVEL MACHINE

12
1
2
3

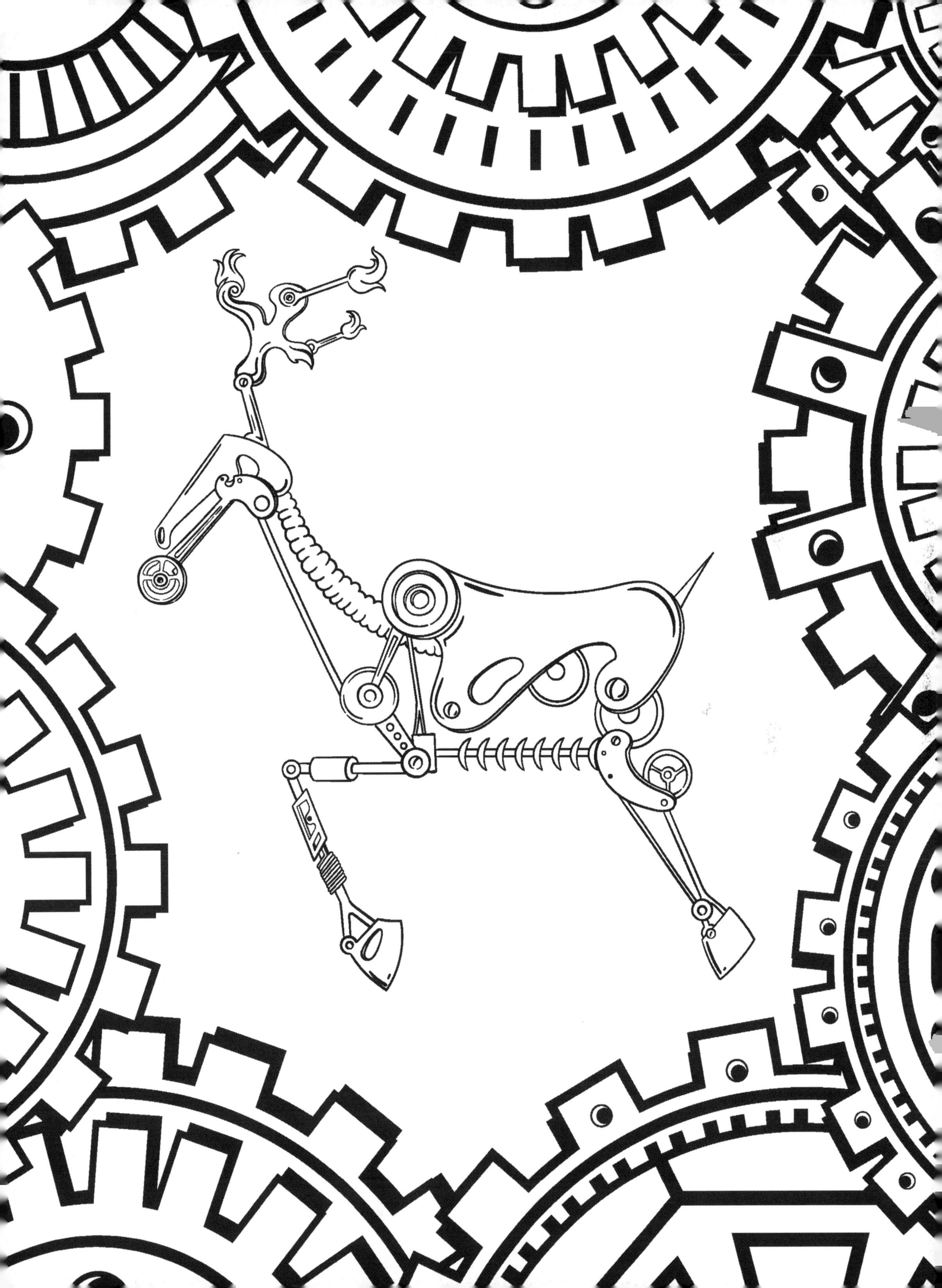

Made in United States
Orlando, FL
10 September 2023

36877048R00061